Yetta M. Goodman • Prisca Martens • Alan D. Flurkev

P9-CDW-279

The
Essential RMA

A Window into Readers' Thinking

RETROSPECTIVE MISCUE ANALYSIS

Richard C. Owen Publishers, Inc.
Katonah, New York

The Essential RMA: A Window into Readers' Thinking

Library of Congress Cataloging-in-Publication
Library of Congress Control Number: 2014941670
ISBN   978-1-57274-900-9 pbk
ISBN   978-1-57274-901-6 ebook

Richard C. Owen Publishers, Inc.
P.O. Box 585
Katonah, New York 10536
914 232-3903
914 232-3977 (fax)
www.RCOwen.com

The text type was set in Times New Roman
Design/production credit: Ginny Tormey, Digital Arts Professional

Printed in the United States of America

9 8 7 6 5 4 3 2 1

For more information about our professional books for teachers and for our children's books, visit our website at www.RCOwen.com or call 1-800-336-5588.

Dedication and Thanks

We dedicate this book on Retrospective Miscue Analysis (RMA)...

...to readers with whom we have worked with RMA and taught us about the reading process while revaluing themselves as confident readers.

...to teachers who use RMA to help their students find it easier and more satisfying to read as a result of talking and thinking collaboratively about their reading.

...to the many reading professionals who read our manuscript and provided important and useful suggestions that contributed to our writing.

...to those who started us along the road to RMA: Chris Worsnop, Ann Alexander (Marek).

...to those who researched and published RMA studies expanding our thinking and knowledge. Often we shared these understandings within the CELT community.

For work especially on this book, we thank Kelly Allen and Debra Goodman. And to Richard Owen who supported us all the way.

Table of Contents

Part III

Preface

When the *Reading Miscue Inventory* (RMI) was first developed in the 1970s, it gave teachers and researchers unprecedented views of reading as a process of making sense of print—what Ken Goodman called "a window on the reading process." Some fifteen years later, when *Retrospective Miscue Analysis* (RMA) was first being used, its potential for helping readers was recognized almost immediately. The initial revelation that learners could actively engage in deep conversations about the reading process and arrive at the same insights as language researchers and teachers led to a second revelation—that RMA could change students' reading in positive ways.

Beginning as an almost casual observation by a middle-school teacher to Yetta Goodman that seventh graders could indeed *do* miscue analysis themselves, Yetta's skepticism was quickly transformed into an energetic research agenda in which RMA evolved along two paths: as a research protocol and as a set of strategy lessons designed to support the development of readers. Those efforts resulted in the publication of *Retrospective Miscue Analysis: Revaluing Readers and Reading* by Yetta Goodman and Ann Marek (1996), a collection of articles by teachers and researchers about readers who learned to revalue themselves through collaborative RMA conversations.

Since the publication of that work, RMA has continued to be used by teachers, students, and researchers for a variety of purposes. And we continue to learn new things about readers and reading as we refine how we conduct RMA strategy lessons, conversations, and engagements with a wide range of age groups. This new, slim volume, *The Essential RMA: A Window into Readers' Thinking*, incorporates those refinements by focusing on the RMA's procedures and its role in supporting the development of proficient reading among children and adults.

Retrospective Miscue Analysis uses miscue analysis as a starting point. But knowing how to do miscue isn't a prerequisite. Although we encourage teachers eventually to learn miscue analysis, it isn't necessary to do a complete miscue analysis to get started. One only needs to record an oral reading, have the desire to hone one's kidwatching skills, and share those observations with a learner.

This book is for teachers who may have little knowledge about miscue analysis, as well as for those who are skilled at doing RMA. It will appeal to those with a range of experiences with RMA, because one of the key strengths of RMA is its *flexibility*. RMA can be done in a face-to-face reading conference or tutoring session, in concurrent small group meetings in a classroom, or with the entire class as part of a language study curriculum. And RMA can be conducted as a student- or teacher-led collaborative discussion.

The Essential RMA: A Window into Readers' Thinking is organized into three parts. Part I introduces the reader to the concepts of miscue analysis and retrospective miscue. Part II is the heart of the book and is comprised of two sections. Section One focuses on miscue analysis procedures such as collecting and analyzing oral reading data, and it provides detailed instructions on how to prepare an RMA session. Section Two provides specific guidelines on how to do RMA, from selecting miscues to organizing conversations in a variety of formats. Part III of *The Essential RMA* explores the use of RMA with different age readers and with groups.

We encourage you to visit *The Essential RMA* website (www. retrospectivemiscue.com), a resource that provides more in-depth knowledge about miscue analysis and RMA, when you are ready to dig deeper. There are links to forms that make RMA easier, lists of questions and comments that deepen conversations, and references to books and articles that are addressed specifically for different age groups and groupings of readers. There are links to recordings of readers, showing how miscues are marked, the kinds of materials we suggest for readings, and how to select materials for readings. Within the pages of this book you will see an occasional icon (➟✳) that identifies some of the content that is included at the website.

In a time when the constraints placed on teachers seem unbearable, and the pressures to implement uniform curricula and reading instruction that quash the craft and creativity of teaching suffocates teachers and students alike, the use of RMA is indispensable. The authentic language study of RMA—exploration that is done with and by learners in collaboration with their teachers and tutors—has the power to bring back joy in teaching and engagement in learning. Enough to revive good teaching; enough to nourish a learner.

Yetta M. Goodman, Prisca Martens, Alan D. Flurkey

Part I
Opening a Window into Readers' Thinking

Learners in Charge of Reading

As we work with readers, our teaching reflects our belief that the human brain is in charge of its own learning. This transactional view of teaching and learning involves knowing that the brain is always learning (Smith, 1995), and that the role of the teacher is to develop innovative ways to support students' learning in a caring and safe environment. In such settings, learners develop confidence and come to value themselves as readers. And because one of our primary goals is to help readers trust themselves as meaning makers, we focus from the beginning on a specific case.

Tommy: A Reader Who Needs to Revalue

In the course of doing a workshop for special education and reading teachers, Alan Flurkey and his colleague Debra Goodman were introduced to Tommy, a seventh-grade student who agreed enthusiastically to be part of the workshop. This normally effusive student, however, became very anxious and subdued when he was asked to read aloud, retell the story, and then participate in a discussion about his reading. With his head bent, and requiring continued encouragement to speak loudly enough to be recorded, Tommy read *The Sweetest Fig* by Chris Van Allsburg (1993), a story he hadn't seen before.

The next day, after listening to his previous reading and making comments that showed evidence of his comprehending, Tommy had an insight during his conversation with Debra (they were discussing his miscue: He read *the cup board* for *his cupboard* in one sentence on page 21 of the story):

2101   [54.] One evening, Bibot took the second fig from

2102   the ʃcup-board
       his cupboard.   [55.] It would not last forever.

Debra: …All right. When you were reading this the first time—

Tommy: I kinda' screwed up.

Debra: What did you do?

Tommy: I said it wrong.

Debra: What did you say?

Tommy: I said, *"cup'board."*

Debra: What did you say this time?

Tommy: "Cupboard." [pronounced *cubberd*]

Debra: Cupboard. [same pron. as Tommy] And how did you know it this time?

Tommy: I said it slower, then I said it faster.

Debra: Oh, okay. Do you think you were thinking about what that word was?

Tommy: Uh, huh [yes].

Debra: Had you seen this word before?

Tommy: No. I've never seen any people that use it. I have, but they don't use it that much.

Debra: They don't use it in books that much?

Tommy: No.

Debra: What do you call these things in your house?

Tommy: [draws breath] Cabinets.

Debra: Cabinets. And in—

Tommy: [draws breath] That's what I can—I can put in for it! Cabinets!

Debra: Yeah, you could have said "cabinets," is that what you're saying?

Tommy: Yeah. 'Cept that wasn't the word.

Debra: Yeah.

Tommy: I *like* doing this.

Up to this point, Tommy's comments about his reading suggested that he believed he always "screwed up." Under the guidance of a teacher who understands the reading process and the meaning-making capabilities of the human brain, Tommy arrived at a personal insight regarding the use of a strategy that would allow him to substitute one meaningful term for another. When Tommy said, *That's what I can—I can put in for it! Cabinets!* he claimed personal responsibility for his own learning. During an earlier discussion about the possibility of making substitutions that fit the meaning of what he was reading, Tommy said in a rather offhanded, self-satisfied way, *I like doing this,* which he repeats again here. He makes it clear that a shift in his evaluation of himself as a learner has started and he is beginning to revalue himself as a reader.

Learning About Readers and Reading

We have learned about how students learn to read by listening to hundreds of readers with a wide range of ages, proficiencies, languages, and backgrounds. Each time we listen, our knowledge about the reading process grows. By listening thoughtfully, we focus on what students read that we often do not expect. We call these unexpected responses miscues, such as Tommy's substitutions when he read *the cup' board* for *his cupboard*. There have been <u>thousands of *miscue* studies</u> that reveal readers' knowledge about the language they read and what they understand about reading (Brown, K. Goodman, & Marek, 1996).

It is by carefully analyzing miscues and discussing a selected number of them with readers that we have come to understand how the reader's brain responds to the written language of a text and constructs meaning. Miscue analysis has been described as *a window on the reading process* (K. Goodman, 1973; K. Goodman & Y. Goodman, 2014), and it helps teachers to understand how reading works so we are able to think about the process, in general, as we consider what the miscues tell us specifically about the individual reader. We explore the reading process by using miscue analysis as our primary tool of investigation. And years of exploration have led to the development of what Ken Goodman calls "a comprehensive model of reading" (K. Goodman & Y. Goodman, 2011).

Miscue analysis provides procedures to help teachers uncover how people read, understand the reading process, and reveal readers' knowledge about reading, language, and concepts and, as a result, points to practices that support readers. Teachers who know miscue analysis discuss what they learn from miscues with the reader (Martens, Y. Goodman, & Flurkey, 1995). We know that these conversations help readers become more confident and lead them to greater success in reading as they think and talk with others about what they do as they read. By discussing these events, teachers help readers become consciously aware of their reading. Since this process involves readers listening to and talking about the miscues they made during a recently completed oral reading, we call the procedure *Retrospective Miscue Analysis* (RMA). Readers wonder, together with the teacher, why they respond as they do to a particular reading of a text, and come to understand that their reading responses occurred because of their focus on making sense. From our perspective, reading is making sense or constructing meaning, synonymous with comprehension and comprehending. We define *comprehending* as the attention readers give to making sense as they read. We define *comprehension* as the readers' knowledge about the text after they have finished reading. In what follows, we provide the background and procedures of RMA and suggest ways for teachers to discuss the knowledge about language and reading strategies that readers use to make sense. As a result, both teachers and readers come to revalue the reading process (K. Goodman, 2003).

One of our major purposes is to suggest ways to engage readers, especially those who struggle and work hard at reading (Duckett, 2007), in using miscue analysis to revalue their reading—to appreciate their underlying strengths and build new understandings about reading. RMA helps teachers respect the evidence that readers are indeed learning all the time as they transact with rich learning materials and experiences.

Finally, we recognize that a range of educational professionals and other caring adults—reading researchers, teachers, specialists, administrators, support staff, tutors, volunteers, and family members—are involved in reading instruction. We use the term *teacher* to represent all who support readers because the focus here is on instruction and how knowledgeable, thoughtful, and insightful teaching supports readers.

Why Retrospective Miscue Analysis

RMA allows readers to be consciously aware of their reading strategies. It allows them to understand and appreciate their own knowledge of language. This is what we call *revaluing*. We know that with their active brains, young children have been learning language for years before they come to school (Whitmore, Martens, Y. Goodman, & Owocki, 2005). And many, as digital natives, soon learn to access and interact with written information on cell phones, iPads, and other technology. Once we understand this key premise, it is easy to appreciate how our brains work and the power of readers' language use. We support children in learning to read by using the strategies and knowledge they already possess as speakers and listeners and observers of their worlds and as a result of their daily transactions with literacy, technology, and a range of multimodal devices.

RMA gives readers opportunities to observe and evaluate their responses to written texts. It empowers them to talk about their reading process with knowledgeable readers. And at the same time, RMA provides evaluative evidence for the teacher about the ways readers respond to their own miscues and the texts they read, and shows the degree to which a conscious awareness of miscues influences reading development. The evidence is used to plan instructional experiences for an individual student, a group of students, or the whole class (Y. Goodman, Watson, and Burke, 1996, 2005).

The Miscue Concept

Before we discuss RMA procedures, we expand on the concept of *miscue*. Because reading is the active construction of meaning, readers use predicting and interpreting strategies. Their active involvement results in making miscues. Essentially, a miscue is any response during oral reading that differs from what a listener would expect to hear. Miscues are often substitutions, such as Tommy's substitution for *cupboard*. They involve omissions, insertions, and reversals. Miscues occur in phrases and across sentence boundaries and show, through complex intonational and grammatical shifts, how readers engage with the text. We provide examples of miscues throughout this book. Miscues reveal how readers comprehend text, expose their points of view, and provide insight into readers' knowledge and experiences. Based on our work with a range of readers, we know that *all readers make miscues* and that miscues are inherent for readers of *all proficiencies*. We emphasize this because miscues are necessary for comprehension; they are part of the reading process.

Comprehension is central to the reading process, and there is *no* reading without comprehension. In fact, we assume that readers are comprehending whenever they read. By involving readers in retelling and through our RMA conversations, we discover why readers transacting with the same text understand it in different ways (Y. Goodman, 1982). As they engage in constructing meaning (making sense), readers use the same <u>reading strategies</u>: sampling, selecting, predicting, confirming, disconfirming, and inferencing. At the same time, readers are using their knowledge of the <u>language cueing systems</u> of graphophonics, grammar (syntax), semantics, and pragmatics (Y. Goodman et al., 2005, Chapter 2, pp. 23-42). Through RMA conversations, we come to understand a lot about what readers do and what they know.

Part II
Retrospective Miscue Analysis:
General Procedures

RMA is a conversation between an experienced reader (a teacher or other students) and reader(s) about what people do and think as they read. RMA conversations occur in one-on-one settings, in small groups, or with a whole class.

We begin with the premise that all readers are thinkers, and that what readers do is a product of that thinking process. As we read, we wonder about the author and make inferences about characters and events. And when we are not sure about what we are reading, we use various reading strategies to solve our problems and expand our growing conceptualizations. We predict what we believe the author means, and we confirm our predictions as we continue reading. We question the author and evaluate the truth of what we are reading. We create images in our heads as we live the experiences the reading awakens in us. And the meanings we make continually change throughout the reading of a text. Those meanings shift with the sense we are making at any given moment. All readers employ such strategies from their earliest days of using oral language as they learn about their social worlds in communication with others. As teachers, we explore this critical thinking with readers through RMA so they become aware of the *control* they have over their own thinking and reading processes and discover the reading strategies they use and their knowledge of language and its cueing systems.

At first, RMA seems complicated, because it requires advanced planning, some basic knowledge of miscue analysis, and an understanding of language. But once underway, the conversations flow easily and become informative and satisfying. And as one gains experience doing RMA, planning becomes more efficient and the implementation becomes more intuitive.

The following two sections explain how to do RMA. Section One is about the Reading Miscue Inventory (RMI) oral reading session, and Section Two is about the RMA sessions. What follows is a quick look at each section.

Section One Quick Look—The Reading Miscue Inventory Oral Reading Session

---

The RMI includes the following parts:

- Before:

    o Thoughtfully select the material to be read.

    o Establish rapport and get to know the reader (Burke Reading Interview).

- During:

    o Conduct the oral reading session (collect miscues and check for *comprehending*).

    o Get a retelling immediately following the oral reading (check for *comprehension*).

- After:

    o Listen to the recording to verify the miscues.

    o Analyze the reading and retelling.

    o Select the miscues for the RMA sessions.

Section Two Quick Look—The Retrospective Miscue Analysis Session

The RMA includes the following parts:

- Before:
    - Select the miscues from the oral reading session (RMI) for the RMA sessions.

    - Develop a discussion plan by filling out the RMA Session Organizer.

    - Collect materials to be used in the discussion:

        - The RMA Session Organizer.

        - An audio or video recording of the oral reading.

        - The original story or article that was read.

        - The teacher's marked typescript (or marked photocopy) of the reading.

        - A blank typescript (or photocopy of the reading) that allows readers to mark their own miscues as they listen to the reading played back.

    - Select a new text for the oral reading for the subsequent RMA session (if appropriate).

- During:
    - Play back the selected miscues for the reader.

    - Encourage the reader to mark his/her miscues on the blank typescript or photocopy.

    - Conduct the RMA discussion using the RMA questions as a guide.

- After:
    - If appropriate, collect another RMI with a new text you have selected.

Section One: The Reading Miscue Inventory (RMI) Oral Reading Session

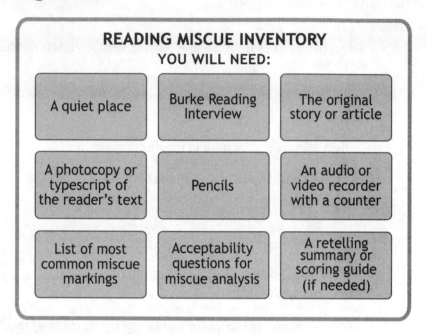

To prepare for the RMA, we first get to know the reader and involve him/her in reading a carefully selected, whole, unfamiliar story or article, followed by a retelling. It is helpful to have a comfortable and quiet place in which to read. We usually sit at a table next to the reader so we have room to spread out the equipment and materials. We make audio (or video) recordings of all of our interactions. Because the teacher's attention is so focused on the reader, important information is sometimes missed without a good recording. Because we want to document as much reader information as possible, we mark the miscues during the reading. After the oral reading, we relisten to the recording to analyze the miscue quality, mark additional miscues we may have missed, and use information from the retelling to help expand our discussions with readers. We use this opportunity to select appropriate miscues to discuss during RMA sessions.

Establishing Rapport and Getting to Know the Reader

At the beginning of the RMI session before the oral reading, teachers interview readers to learn about their backgrounds, and their views about reading and themselves as readers. To understand the readers' perceptions about reading, we use questions from the <u>Burke Reading Interview</u> (Y. Goodman et al. 2005, pp. 273–274, and Appendix A). (Also see <u>Burke Interview Modified for Older Readers</u> <u>(BIMOR)</u>, Y. Goodman et al. pp. 275–276, and Appendix B, and the <u>Entrevista</u> <u>Burke</u> [Burke Interview translated into Spanish], Appendix C.) Here are some of the questions:

- What do you do when you come to *something* you don't know?

  o Followed by: What else do you do? (We intentionally use "something" because the readers' responses provide insights into whether readers focus on words, ideas, comprehension, etc.)

- Who is a good reader you know?

- What makes (Robin) a good reader?

- Do you think (Robin) ever comes to something he/she doesn't know?

  o "Yes": What do you think (Robin) does?

  o "No": Pretend (Robin) does come to something he/she does not know. What do you think he/she would do?

- What do you do well as a reader?

- What are the favorite things you read? Or who is your favorite author?

Learning about readers' perceptions of reading, how the reading process works, who is a good reader, and what readers do when they encounter difficulties gives insights into how readers conceptualize reading. For example, some readers state that they *sound out* when they come to something they don't know, and that good readers read fast and accurately and never encounter difficulties. These readers conceive of reading as a word-oriented process in which *reading* means saying all the words accurately. On the other hand, readers who state that they are good readers because they *understand what they read* indicate that they conceptualize reading as a *process of constructing meaning.* The patterns of miscues produced by these readers tend to corroborate what they say they believe about reading (although sometimes what readers say they do and what they really do when reading differ considerably).

When we work with biliterate readers or readers who live in bilingual communities, we ask similar questions about any other languages they read or use orally. Often, readers report using strategies when they read in their first or more proficient language in different ways than when they read English. A discussion about these differences helps teachers increase readers' awareness of using different reading strategies for different reading contexts. Even young biliterate readers are able to articulate differences between the languages they know and read. We ask older and adult readers <u>additional questions</u> to get at their views about their history of reading instruction and to explore the kinds of materials they read or want to read.

We add questions to the Burke Interview if needed to gain insight into readers' perceptions about reading and about themselves as readers to fit the ages, linguistic backgrounds, and experiences of the specific readers with whom we are working. We use this information in our conversations to help them understand the value of focusing on meaning construction (comprehending and comprehension) while reading. We pose similar questions a number of times across various RMA sessions to document readers' changes in attitudes. We also ask these questions (especially before the *first* RMI) to establish rapport. Being asked to read aloud, especially by a teacher, may provoke anxiety in some readers. By asking open-ended, judgment-free questions in a relaxed, conversational manner in which the stated goal is to learn more about the reader, we build trust, reduce anxiety, and support the reader's confidence. A trusting, safe environment is essential for successful RMA sessions.

Selecting Material for RMI

It is useful to have a selection of stories or articles on hand that are within the language and conceptual knowledge of the reader, but which are also somewhat challenging. Teachers often set aside a range of both fiction and nonfiction reading material ready for use, although there are times when teachers invite readers to select the material they would like to read and talk about during RMA.

<u>Selecting material</u> needs to be done thoughtfully (Appendix D). It is helpful

for the teacher to know the reader's background, interests, and confidence level. Although the text is unfamiliar to the reader, the content should relate to the reader's experiences, and it should be written in language that is comfortable for the reader (Mooney, 2004). At the same time, the text should be challenging enough to result in approximately 25 miscues to establish a pattern, but not so difficult that the reader is unable to read the material independently. The more we know about the reader's background and interests, the easier it is to select appropriate material. Standardized reading tests often underestimate the reader's ability.

For RMI purposes, it is necessary to select an entire cohesive printed text (story, article, or chapter with a beginning, middle, and ending) that is interesting and well written. The length of the text may vary considerably, depending upon the age and proficiency of the reader, but it is most useful if passages are at least 500 words long. Since miscue research has shown that the quality of miscues changes after the first 200 words in a text (Menosky, 1971), it is critical that texts be long enough to allow readers to become immersed in the material to demonstrate their most effective and efficient strategies.

Usually, as a result of readers' comprehending, the patterns of miscues begin to shift as they become familiar with the content and the writing style: Their predictions become more effective, they self-correct more miscues that do not make sense, they make fewer corrections on miscues that retain syntactic and semantic acceptability, and the miscues that bear high graphic (visual) similarity with the text decrease. In short, they produce more *high-quality* miscues (miscues that do not disrupt meaning) and correct those miscues that do disrupt meaning. These shifts across the text provide evidence of the readers' comprehending strategies that ultimately result in the readers' comprehension. This provides evidence for the metaphor of miscues being a window on the reading process.

We define a sentence as being syntactically acceptable if it follows what we all *intuitively* understand as the "rules" of English. Those rules cover word order, tense, number, and gender. If a sentence "sounds" like English, we judge it to be syntactically acceptable even if it contains "nonwords." A sentence read as *Judy shrickled and jumped up on her chair* for *Judy shrieked and jumped up on her chair* is a syntactically acceptable structure. Even though *shrickled* is not a word in English, it is in the same place and has the same ending as a past tense verb. We define a sentence as being semantically acceptable if it is a *meaningful* sentence in the context of the story being read. *Judy shrickled and jumped on her chair* is syntactically acceptable but not semantically acceptable, due to the nonword substitution of *shrickled* for *shrieked*.

The following examples, taken from a fourth grader's reading of the children's book *Winnie the Witch* (Thomas & Paul, 2007), illustrate shifts that occur as meaning is built across a text. Keep in mind that the reader is not given any help while reading. The numbers prior to the sentences indicate the sentence number in the text. The nonword miscue *$campet* in sentence 4 is eventually read as the expected response *carpet* in sentences 33 and 49, and the miscue *magical* in sentence 19 shifts to the expected response *magic* in sentence 44. (Note that we place a "$" before a nonword to indicate that it is not a word in English).

[3.] The house was black on the outside and black on

the inside.   [4.] The (UC) $campet / cam- / cer- (carpet) was black.   [5.] The chairs were black.

[33.] Now, Winnie could see Wilbur when he sat (*lie*) on a chair,

when he lay on the carpet, and when he crawled into the grass.

[49.] The chairs were white with red

and white (C) *sheets / ch-* cushions.   [50.] The (C) *car-pet* carpet

was green with pink roses.

[19.] She picked up her *magical* magic wand.

[44.] She waved her magic wand and…

In sentence 4, the reader reads *The cer- cam- campet was black….* The hyphens indicate a partial attempt: (*cer* sounds like *sir*, which shows that *c* can be pronounced as an *s*). The reader then says *cam-* (another partial attempt) and then $*campet*, both starting with a /k/ sound. This shows the reader's knowledge of the relation between *c* and *s* and that the reader knows that *ca* at the beginning of a word is usually pronounced /k/. The *uc* in a circle indicates three uncorrected attempts. The reading of this sentence results in a syntactically acceptable sentence (sounds like an English sentence), although the nonword $*campet* renders the sentence unacceptable semantically because the sentence doesn't make sense in the story. The lengths of the lines under the words indicate how far the reader repeated. The *c* in a circle indicates self-correction. A word written over the printed text shows substitutions *lie* for *sat*, *sheets* for *cushions*, and *magical* for *magic*.

Over time, teachers develop sets of the original material and have typescripts ready to use with a variety of readers in terms of proficiency and interests. Children's and adolescents' magazines and old basal readers include short, interesting fiction and nonfiction selections. Plays, short stories, and folktales also work well with a wide range of readers. We avoid overly simplistic single-sentence or one-word-on-a-page texts, even for very young readers; while these sorts of texts may seem simple, the inauthentic language they use often makes reading more difficult. We are well aware that the power of the text has a great influence in engaging readers (Meek, 1988). Note that if teachers are interested in research, publication, and presentation of any of this work, it is important to know copyright issues when selecting materials for reading.

Recording the Oral Reading

We label all materials with the reader's name and date. (Digital recording devices are well suited for RMI and RMA. A digital sound file allows the teacher to find specific places in the recording with great precision.) Materials to have on hand for the oral reading include:

- A blank typescript or photocopy of the reader's text on which the teacher marks miscues and takes notes.

- An outline or notes about the written material for the teacher to use during the retelling.

- A recording device (audio recorder, video recorder, smart phone, etc., to record the session for later analysis and for use during the RMA session).

- Pencils to easily edit markings and make changes when relistening to the recordings. We use pencils because we may hear different things with each subsequent listening to a recording. If we make notations in ink and need to make changes we get a messy typescript. If we make markings in pencil we can erase. We often use different colored pencils to mark different phenomena.

- Notepad or paper to make notes about the reading and the retelling.

Before the reader begins we conduct the reading interview and seek to establish a rapport. We ask the reader to state their name (or the pseudonym they have been invited to select) and date into the recorder. We explain the purpose of the session and why we are recording. We then hand them the selected book, chapter, or article and give the following instructions:

> *"Please read this story (chapter, article) out loud. If you come to something you don't know, do what you would do if you were reading alone. Since we want to know how you read on your own, I won't give you any help while you're reading. When you finish reading, I'll ask you to tell me what you've read, and then we'll talk about the story (or article) and how you think you read it. I'm recording your reading and retelling, so you can listen to yourself next time we meet and we talk about what you do as a reader. I'm also taking notes as you read, and I'll share them with you."*

The reader may also find it reassuring that this is not a "test" and there are no grades involved. While it is not crucial that these instructions be given exactly as worded above, it is important that the essence be shared with the reader; that is, that the reading will be *uninterrupted*, with the teacher providing *no help*, and that a discussion of what the text was about will follow.

During the reading, the teacher marks the miscues (see next section) on a copy of the material while the reader is reading orally. On rare occasions when a reader seems overly nervous about the miscue marking, the teacher may wait and mark miscues later. Since text lines are close together, the teacher often <u>prepares a</u> <u>typescript</u> to mark during the reading that is triple-spaced and uses the same line and page endings as the original material to examine how formatting influences the reader. If there is enough space between the lines in the original text, some teachers use photocopies of the original to mark miscues and make notes.

If readers stop reading for an extended time (more than about 30 seconds), we ask what they would do if they were reading by themselves. We assure them that whatever strategy they choose is acceptable, and remind them that they can omit or keep on reading. Because we want to see what readers do when they are reading alone, we never prompt them or give them the word.

Marking Miscues

Miscues become visible during oral reading when what the teacher hears (the observed response) is different from what the teacher expects to hear (the expected response). Readers use the same reading process when their observed responses match the expected responses (no evidence of miscues) as they do when they make miscues. However, it is only through listening carefully and marking the miscues that teachers have authentic documentation of the readers' strategies and language knowledge.

In order to analyze miscues and to explore them with students during RMA, we adapted a <u>notation system</u> for marking miscues based on procedures used in original miscue analysis research (see Appendix E). By using common notations, teachers who are not present for the original reading can still understand the reader's responses when they examine the marked typescript. There are examples throughout that show miscue markings. The numbers at the left margin are called the *line address*. The first two numbers indicate the page of the original text, and the second two numbers indicate the line on that page. Line address 0714 means page 7, line 14 of the original text. Keeping the line breaks in the typescript in the same place as in the original text provides information about how readers move from one line to another and how sentence and line endings and beginnings influence the reading of the text. There are also times when we number each sentence sequentially.

0713   Ⓒ
ⓒ I turned ᵗᵒ a sharp corner, and the apples rolled⌐all over the floor of the   Ⓒ a-

0714   car. I looked down to see if I could kick some ⟨of the⟩ apples from under

0715   my feet.

Lines 0713–0715 show miscue markings for two substitutions with self-corrections, and an omission of two words (circled). In this example, a 14-year-old reads line 0713 as *I turned to—* (immediate self-correction with a repetition back to the beginning of the sentence) ... *I turned a sharp corner and the apples rolled a—* (/aw/ is a partial response with an immediate self-correction) ... *all over the floor of the car.* In 0714, he omits the words *of the* and continues to the end of the sentence on line 0715, reading, *I looked down to see if I could kick some apples from under my feet.* The markings show a pattern of high-quality miscues that results in acceptable sentences both semantically and syntactically with no change of meaning to the story. We say more about the coding below.

1312   They are old and have ₍ₐ₎ little ^money.

In line 1312, a 9-year-old reader inserts *a* before *little* and *money* after *little*. This sentence was read as *They are old and have a little money.* The result is an acceptable sentence with partial meaning change to the story. Substitution miscues are indicated by writing the reader's response directly over the word of the text. Substitutions include nonwords and reversals. Insertions are indicated by writing a proofreader's carat between two words and writing the insertion miscue directly above it. Omissions are indicated by circling the word that was omitted by the reader. We also document misarticulations, dialect, second language variations, partial responses, and pauses over 5 seconds; these are not counted as miscues, but we want to see how they influence the reader. We underline repetitions according to the length of the repeated text and indicate whether they are corrected (*C* in a circle), reread with no changes (*R* in a circle), or unsuccessfully corrected (*UC* in a circle). The underlines with appropriate codes make the readers' strategies visible. We also write notes in the margin of the typescript that include useful observations for follow-up discussions (i.e., finger pointing, subvocalizing, perusal of illustrations, and oral asides; see Appendix F).

The Retelling and Its Analysis

When students finish reading, we make supportive comments, thanking them and asking for a retelling, which is recorded. The retelling is in two parts: the *unaided retelling* followed by an *aided retelling*. We initiate the unaided retelling by saying to the reader, "Tell me everything you remember about what you just read." We encourage the reader to continue without interruption, and as the reader retells, we make notes, jotting down the reader's language as we do so. Our notes remind us what we plan to discuss with the reader during the aided retelling, and, by using the reader's language, remind us of the reader's responses for use in subsequent RMA sessions. We transition into the aided retelling by asking the reader open-ended questions based on information already shared.

- Tell me more about that (a specific incident the reader mentioned).

- Why do you think (character) did that?

- What happened before (or after) a specific event?

- Why did the author want you to know about that?

In this way, we encourage extended responses and gather more specific information about the reader's comprehension. When conducting the aided retelling, we use the same pronunciations for names and words as our reader, and we do not introduce new information about the story that was not first mentioned by the reader, although we do ask open-ended questions that might lead the reader to provide additional information. While oral retellings are the most common, depending on the teacher's purposes, written retellings, sketches, time lines, collages, etc., are useful with readers who are reluctant to retell orally, and they often work better with informational materials (Siegel, 1991; Whitin, 1996).

Since all reading is interpretative, retellings reveal what readers choose to share at a particular time. We, therefore, never assume that retellings represent readers' full understanding. Readers continue to extend their comprehension during retelling as well as during the RMA session (Y. Goodman et al., 2005).

We assess the retelling by relating readers' statements and inferences to the plot, theme, and characters in a story, and by noting readers' concepts and misconceptions, especially in nonfiction material. When teachers use the same stories or articles with many students, it is useful to develop a <u>retelling summary</u> of the story or article. This helps the teacher encourage the readers to *say more* about what they read during the aided retelling.

Some teachers use a holistic score (1–5) to indicate the completeness of the retelling. It can be used across readings to show the reader's developing abilities with retelling. Since we often use more difficult stories throughout the RMA sessions, it is important to keep in mind that retelling scores reflect the challenge of the newer reading material, so we do not expect scores to always be higher for each new reading. Retelling information is useful during the subsequent RMA discussions as readers talk about their understandings of the text.

Analyzing Miscues and Selecting Miscues for the RMA Session

Before analyzing the readers' miscues, we listen again to the recording to verify the markings on the typescript to create an accurate representation of what we have heard. We examine readers' marked typescripts to find patterns of miscues, and to learn about readers' strengths and needs (Y. Goodman & Marek, 1996).

To determine the degree to which readers display concern for comprehension and comprehending as they read, we analyze each sentence of the typescript. Teachers should develop experience with the coding of sentences before they involve readers in the process. We read each sentence with all miscues *as finally produced by the reader.* Each sentence gets asked three questions: for *syntactic acceptability*, one for *semantic acceptability*, and one for *meaning change.* And depending on the teacher's judgment, each sentence could be coded with **Y** for Yes, **N** for No, **P** for Partial.

Question 1 asks Is the sentence *syntactically acceptable?* In other words, is the sentence acceptable in terms of its grammar–are all the parts of the speech in place–or, does it sound like it has an acceptable English word order? Some "incomplete" or "fragment" sentences can be coded as acceptable, too, if the teacher believes it has acceptable English, as does the second sentence from the following excerpt of *Winnie the Witch* (Thomas & Paul, 2007, pp. 12-13): But

Wilbur was not allowed to sleep on the bed...so Winnie put him outside. Outside in the grass. This question is coded either **Y** or **N**.

Question 2 asks Is the sentence *semantically acceptable?* In other words, is the sentence *meaningful* in the context of the story or article? Does it make sense? This question is also coded either **Y** or **N**.

Question 3 asks To what degree does the sentence (with the miscues as the reader left them) change the meaning of the story or article? This question can be coded **N**, **Y**, or **P**.

Some rules: Question 1 (syntax) can be coded either **Y** or **N**. If it is coded **Y**, then we continue on to Question 2 (semantics). But if Question 1 is coded **N** (*not* syntactically acceptable), then we automatically code Question 2 **N** (*not* semantically acceptable), and skip Question 3 (meaning change) entirely. We use a dash "–" to indicate Question 3 was skipped. The resulting code would be **NN-**. In other words, Question 2 cannot be coded "higher" than Question 1, and both Questions 1 & 2 must be coded **Y** before we can ask Question 3.

Something else to consider: it is possible to code Question 1 **Y** and Question 2 **N**. This usually happens when a sentence contains a nonword miscue that retains the same grammar as the word in the text. But because we don't consider nonwords to be meaningful, we code the sentence **N** for Question 2. The code would be **YN-**. And like the example above, if Question 2 is coded **N**, then Question 3 is skipped ("–"). We only move on to Question 3 if first two questions have been coded **Y**.

There is a fourth question, but it is not a sentence-level question. Question 4 asks the degree to which an individual miscue looks like the text for which it was substituted. A detailed description of each question and how to use it is shown below.

Procedure and Questions for Coding

Setup:

- Mark the miscues carefully and listen to the recording a second time if necessary.

- Number all of the sentences in the story sequentially, writing the number prior to each sentence.

- Move down the typescript with a ruler, stopping at each period. In the margin to the right of the typescript, make a line on which to put your coding (responses to Question 1 are placed in the first position, responses for Question 2 are in the second position, and responses to Question 3 are in the third position).

- Prior to the line, write the number that corresponds to the sentence number in the typescript.

Example:

0101   [1.] Doctor De Soto, the dentist, did very good work, so he had no

0102   end of patients. [2.] Those close to his own size-moles, chipmunks,   1. _YYN_

0103   et cetera-sat in the regular dentist's chair.   2. _YYN_

Coding:

- Read each sentence with the miscues the way the reader finally left them.

- Evaluate each sentence according to these questions:

Question 1: *Syntactic Acceptability*

Is the sentence syntactically acceptable in the reader's dialect and within the context of the entire selection?

Yes—The sentence, as finally produced by the reader, is syntactically acceptable.

No—The sentence, as finally produced by the reader, is not syntactically acceptable.

Syntactic acceptability relates to the grammar of the sentence, such as parts of speech, pronoun references, word order, tense, number, etc. We consider whether the sentence sounds like English. (Miscue analysis can be done in any written language, and in such cases "acceptability" is considered in relation to the language being read.)

Sentence 1 (see example above) is syntactically acceptable. The final version of the sentence is, *Doctor De Sto, the dentist, did good work, so he had no end of patients*. Note that the nonword *destense* was self-corrected, that the omission of *very* was not corrected, and that *De Sto* was not corrected. Because the final version of this sentence contains all of the parts of speech expected in an English sentence, the sentence is judged to be an appropriate English sentence as the reader finally left it. (Code **Y** for Yes in first position.)

Question 2: *Semantic Acceptability*

Is the sentence semantically acceptable in the reader's dialect and within the context of the entire selection? (Question 2 cannot be coded Y if Question 1 has been coded N.)

Yes—The sentence, as finally produced by the reader, is semantically acceptable.

No—The sentence, as finally produced by the reader, is not semantically acceptable.

Semantic acceptability refers to the meaning and content in English sentences: Does it still make sense within the context of the selection?

Sentence 1 (in the above example) is semantically acceptable. In other words, the final version of the sentence *Doctor De Sto, the dentist, did good work, so he had no end of patients,* is meaningful in this story. (Code **Y** for Yes in second position.)

Question 3: *Meaning Change*

Does the sentence, as finally produced by the reader, change the meaning of the selection? (Question 3 is coded only if both Questions 1 & 2 are coded Y.)

No—There is no change in the meaning of the selection.

Partial—There is inconsistency, loss, or change of a *minor* idea, incident, character, fact, sequence, or concept in the selection.

Yes—There is inconsistency, loss, or change of a *major* idea, incident, character, fact, sequence, or concept in the selection.

Sentence 1 results in no meaning change. This is a fiction story, so the name of the character is not significant to its meaning. The omission of *very* (an intensifier) has minimal impact on the meaning and does not change the sentence's meaning in the story. Code **N** for No meaning change in the third position. Some might argue that there is partial meaning change. The coder makes a determination based on the influences of these miscues on the whole story or article.

Question 4: *Graphic Similarity*

How much does the miscue look like the text item?

H—High degree of graphic similarity exists between the miscue and the text.

S—Some degree of graphic similarity exists between the miscue and the text.

N—No degree of graphic similarity exists between the miscue and the text.

There are two substitution miscues in the above example: *Sto* for *Soto* and a nonword that sounds like $destense. We would code *Sto* for *Soto* as **H** (a high degree of look-alike similarity). For the nonword substitution, we would code graphic similarity as **H** (high degree of similarity). When two thirds of the substitution is similar, we code **H**; when one third is similar, we code **S**, and when *nothing* is similar, we code **N**. We place letters **H**, **S**, or **N** near the miscue to record these codings.

Coding Patterns that Show the Results for Miscue Quality

There are five possible coding choices for any given sentence (**YYN, YYP, YYY, YN–,** and **NN–**). The first three codings (**YYN, YYP,** and **YYY**) indicate "language strength", because the miscues are high quality or are self-corrected. The remaining two codings (**YN–** and **NN–**) show weakness that result from low-quality miscues.

Sentences marked **YYN** are the result of high-quality substitution, omission, and insertion miscues that are acceptable in the sentence or involve proficient use of correction strategies. **YYP** sentences indicate that the miscues are high quality but they change the meaning of the passage to a partial degree. This information is important when teachers select miscues to use for RMA sessions. **YYY** sentences include miscues that result in syntactically and semantically acceptable sentences although they make major changes to the meaning of the text. Sentences with **YN** patterns (syntactically acceptable but not semantically acceptable) and sentences with **NN** patterns (syntactically unacceptable and semantically unacceptable) are the result of low-quality miscues that disrupt meaning. Checking the graphic similarity of the miscue substitutions in such sentences provides insight into the reader's reliance on graphic cues (visual information).

NOTE: Every sentence is coded in this procedure (even those in which no miscue is produced). A sentence in which no miscue is produced receives a coding of YYN, meaning the sentence is syntactically and semantically acceptable with no meaning change. Taking into consideration all the sentences readers produce without miscues helps us understand how it is possible for readers to make many miscues and still comprehend and retell the text successfully. It is important to examine the areas of text where readers make no miscues to further expand on understanding the efficient and effective strategies readers use.

This discussion may seem complicated, especially for those who have had little or no experience with miscue analysis, but we encourage you to *play around* with the systematic marking and coding of miscue analysis. Just get started. We know that the more opportunities teachers have to listen to readers in this way, the easier it becomes to mark and code miscues. Teachers soon develop expert "miscue ears". And at *The Essential RMA* website, you will be able to further explore miscue analysis and RMA, and find additional support to help you.

You might highlight the sentences with miscues that you believe are acceptable (**YYN, YYP,** and **YYY**) and the ones that are not (**YN-** and **NN-**) in two different colors. Leave the sentences without miscues without any highlighting. This provides a visual picture of the influence of miscues on reading. It shows the degree to which your readers are making sense. Even without a lot of background, when two or more teachers work together, they figure out the degrees of acceptability by exploring together the influence of miscues on readers' comprehension. In any case, if you are not in a position to analyze the miscues, we still encourage you to continue exploring RMA following the procedures outlined in the subsequent sections.

Selecting Miscues for RMA Sessions

For RMA purposes, especially during our initial conversations with our readers, we look for high-quality miscues that result in semantically and syntactically acceptable sentences. These would include appropriate self-corrections that reflect language strength (**YYN** and **YYP** patterns). Patterns of high-quality miscues indicate readers who are problem solving—working at making sense and using efficient and effective strategies flexibly. Making acceptable substitutions and omissions, predicting possible miscues that are not acceptable, and self-correcting are the kinds of miscues and strategies we select for RMA discussions. When we talk with readers about their high-quality miscues, we help them recognize what they are already doing that shows their focus is on making sense.

The miscues selected for RMA can come from anywhere in the typescript and be sequenced in any order that the teacher considers appropriate. In our conversations, we first highlight strategies that show readers' strengths (sentences coded **YYN** and **YYP**) because this puts them at ease and helps teachers build a trusting relationship. Although RMA is valuable for all readers, it is often used with readers who do not consider themselves very good readers. It is helpful for readers to realize that, in addition to problems they know they have, they also are using effective strategies as documented by high-quality miscues. We have learned that when readers see that their miscues show their effective use of reading strategies and their knowledge of language, it challenges their perceptions of themselves as readers in trouble, and as a result, *they revalue themselves and discover new confidence.* These readers are rarely in situations where they are asked to discuss their own positive influences on their reading and to examine the smart things they do as they read. RMA provides them with opportunities to do just that.

The teacher uses what is learned about the reader from miscue analysis, the retelling, and information from the reading interview, and thoughtfully selects about five miscues to plan for the first RMA session. It is helpful to have a <u>RMA Session Organizer</u> to list the miscues that will be discussed, indicate why they were chosen, and where to locate them on the typescript and on the recording (Appendix G). Teachers should adapt the organizer to fit their purposes. After becoming comfortable with RMA, during subsequent RMA sessions, the teacher may invite readers to mark their own miscues on the blank typescript or to stop the taping when they hear a miscue, so that the teacher and student can mark the miscues together on a blank transcript.

Teachers are sometimes surprised to discover that even beginning readers have sophisticated ideas about how written language works and what they are trying to do as they read. Readers are eager to talk about their own language, the language of the text, and what they believe reading is all about. They thoughtfully discuss their insights about their reading strategies. Readers have both conceptions and misconceptions about the reading process, and the more opportunities they have to discuss their reading in a serious way with an interested adult or in a small group of interested peers, the more articulate they become about the nature of reading. The kinds of responses readers make during our RMA conversations reveal readers' metalinguistic and metacognitive knowledge. That means that they are able to talk and think about language and their thinking processes in an abstract way. Using what we have learned by analyzing readers' miscues, and with insights from their retellings and the reading interview we are now ready for the RMA revaluing sessions.

Section Two: Retrospective Miscue Analysis (RMA) Sessions

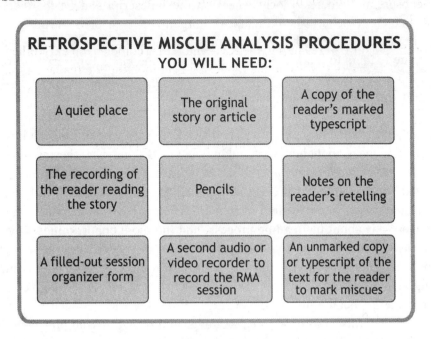

RETROSPECTIVE MISCUE ANALYSIS PROCEDURES
YOU WILL NEED:

A quiet place	The original story or article	A copy of the reader's marked typescript
The recording of the reader reading the story	Pencils	Notes on the reader's retelling
A filled-out session organizer form	A second audio or video recorder to record the RMA session	An unmarked copy or typescript of the text for the reader to mark miscues

Interactions During the RMA Sessions

To begin the RMA session, we keep in mind the importance of the dynamic relationship between teacher and student as they explore and revalue the reading process together. Revaluing (K. Goodman, 2003) recognizes and validates the linguistic strengths and reading strategies that all readers possess as they work at making sense of print. Goodman writes:

> [Students] must revalue the process of reading as the construction of meaning in response to print. They must come to appreciate their own strengths, to recognize the productive strategies they already can use, and to build positively on those. They must come to put in perspective their transactions with authors through texts. Then they can put proper value on themselves and understand that no one easily reads and comprehends everything and that what one knows before reading constrains what one can know after reading. They need to know that some texts are difficult because they are poorly written, and others are difficult because they

contain new, complex ideas.... Finally, they need to realize that the easiest things to read are going to be the very ones that they have the most interest in and the most background for and from which they get the most pleasure. (p. 17)

For the purpose of revaluing, the RMI and RMA complement each other. The RMI allows teachers to revalue the reader by documenting the reader's problem-solving strategies. RMA is a series of conversations that provide opportunities for teachers and readers to share observations of the readers' strengths over time—their problem-solving strategies as they read—and to consciously converse about what the reader's smart brain does during the reading process.

The RMA Sessions

In this section, we focus on one-on-one teacher–student interactions and later discuss alternative uses of small group and whole class RMA.

To conduct an RMA session, it is important to have the following materials on hand:

- Audio or video recorder for playing back selected miscues for the reader to hear and talk about.

- Second recorder to capture the RMA session. This is optional, but since RMA conversations frequently result in reader insights and "Aha!" moments, we recommend recording the session to share with parents, teachers, and other interested stakeholders. It is especially useful if the teacher wants to do some research, write an article or present a workshop about the RMA experience

- Reader's text (original book, chapter, or article).

- Notes from the reader's retelling to remind the teacher of the reader's concepts, language, and knowledge.

- Marked typescript or photocopy of the original reading.

- Unmarked typescript or photocopy of the text for the reader to mark his or her miscues when the reading is played back. This is especially beneficial for later RMA sessions.

- Session organizer form to keep on track during the session and as a record of the session focus (Appendix G1). The session organizer includes the selected miscues and counter numbers, to help find the recorded miscues easily (Appendix G2).

- Pencils for marking miscues and making notes.

We begin the session by sharing, in general terms, readers' effective and efficient strategies that reveal their hard work and indicate what they were doing that good readers typically do. We use the concept of hard work to validate for the reader that we know they are not simply "messin' up." We want them to know we respect that what they are doing takes effort, and we sometimes refer to their responses as *smart miscues* to help define what *we* consider to be productive strategies. We would never use the term *bad reader* or *poor reader*. We explain our rationale for involving them in the RMA process and make clear that we expect them to actively participate. Once the rationale and procedures have been established, the RMA begins:

1. Turn on the second recorder and leave it running during the entire session.

2. Start by locating the sentence in the story or article (the written/printed text) where the first selected miscue(s) will be found when the reader hears himself/ herself on the recording.

3. Ask the reader to read the sentence (either silently or aloud).

4. Ask the reader: "Do you remember what happened when you read this last time?" Follow the reader's comments into a discussion about the sentence or passage.

5. Play the recorded excerpt for the reader.

6. Ask the reader, "Did you notice anything?" If the reader says "no," play the excerpt again. Sometimes, especially in the case of high-quality miscues that aren't corrected, readers don't detect such miscues and may need to hear the segment several times.

7. Once the reader identifies the miscue, discuss how it helped the reader toward making sense of the text.

We often involve the reader in marking miscue(s) in pencil on a copy of the text. We share with readers simple notations for marking miscues that highlight readers' strategies (word-for-word substitutions, omissions and insertions, and self-corrections). Some teachers have a chart of the markings available and encourage the reader to take the lead in <u>marking</u> what they hear. In this way, readers have a sense of ownership in this process. If the reader notices miscues by saying, "I made a mistake here," or "I screwed up," as they often do initially, we remind them that miscues aren't mistakes and that all readers make miscues. We emphasize that readers make high-quality miscues especially when they are thinking about making sense. An effective way to make this point is to play a recording of a proficient reader (a principal reading a morning announcement, a news anchor reading the news, or the teacher reading aloud to the class). Readers should also be invited to note teachers' miscues when they are reading aloud. Readers become comfortable when they realize that proficient readers also make miscues and they are a normal part of the reading process.

Original RMA Guiding Questions.

Once the reader has listened to the sentence and marked the miscue, we invite them to consider their own thinking during reading (comprehending) by asking questions similar to the ones we ask when we analyze the miscues to select them for the RMA (see pp. 21-24). The following are the original RMA questions developed by Y. Goodman & Marek (1996, p. 53):

1. Does the miscue make sense?

2a. Was the miscue corrected?

2b. Should it have been?

Depending on how they are answered, questions 1 and 2 initiate discussions about the non-necessity of self-correcting high quality miscues (1-Yes, 2a-No, 2b-No). These questions also emphasize the importance of self-correcting when meaning is lost (1-No, 2a-Yes, 2b-Yes). If the answer to questions 1 and 2a is "No," then we ask questions that focuses on other cueing systems (graphic and sound similarity) the reader may have used in making the miscue:

3. Does the miscue look like what was on the page?

4. Does the miscue sound like what was on the page?

Questions 5 and 6 raise thinking about the strategies of selecting and predicting to a conscious level:

5. Why do you think you made this miscue?

6. Did that miscue affect your understanding of the text?

NOTE: Questions 3 and 4 about graphic and sound similarity demonstrate readers' phonics knowledge and a "Yes" response to either suggests that readers may be relying more on graphic information than they need to. A teacher's response to miscues that show high graphic or sound similarity might be: "Yes, it looks and/ or sounds like what is in the text. You know the relationship between the system of sounds and print. Now that you know that, can you think of something to make it make sense? How might it become semantically or syntactically acceptable?" Students need to realize that an overreliance on graphic information without a focus on meaning does not lead to comprehension. This is especially true for students who have had lots of subskills reading instruction (K. Goodman & Y. Goodman, 2011; Nelson, Damico, & Smith, 2006).

These and related questions invite readers into the conversation and let them know that we are seriously interested in their reading and their responses. Our conversations demonstrate that talking about miscues and how they read is thought provoking. The questions and follow-up discussions establish a shared language and provide evidence that these conversations evoke metalinguistic awareness. The questions help readers see that they are using what they know about language and reading to make sense. We are actually inviting them to join us as researchers to discover how the reading process works.

Rolando, a 12-year-old Spanish/English bilingual with low reading scores worked with Alan Flurkey during the early development of RMA (Flurkey, 1996, p. 107). Rolando is able to make clear, at approximately his fifth RMA session, what the reading process means to him:

"Mighty much obliged for the favor," he called

as he headed ~~up the trail~~ *from rail* toward home.

Rolando reads: *"Mighty much obliged for the favor," he called as he headed from the rail toward home.*

The substitutions of acceptable miscues *from the rail* for *up the trail* produce a syntactically and semantically acceptable sentence with a major meaning change. Code: **YYY**.

Alan: Did you hear what you said?... headed—

Rolando: *The rail.*

Alan: Okay. Let's look at that.

Rolando: There's a *tr–*, a rail can be a railroad. Can't it be like a barbed-wire fence? A rail…? Like you could hold onto something… Maybe I was really getting into the story and I was imagining stuff. When you are reading, you're supposed to, huh? Then it's like a movie, but you're filming it and you're reading off the parts.

Alan: You said earlier that your dad has horses, right?

Rolando: Yeah, he has a small corral.

Alan: What's that corral made of?

Roland: It's steel—a rail! Instead of *trail*, I put *rail* and *toward* used the ... he was walking toward home—*from the rail toward home.*

What to Expect During an RMA Session

Sometimes, even during the first RMA session, we notice a shift in the readers' self-confidence. They become RMA enthusiasts because they have rarely had the opportunity to engage in serious conversations with a sensitive teacher genuinely interested in hearing what they believe and how they think. They realize there are no expected *single right answers*. Their typical "Oh, I always do stupid things like that" responses diminish, and they make comments such as "I think I liked the way I did it better than in the book" or "I said *front of the tree* instead of *foot of the tree... foot* and *front* meant the same thing. A tree all front because it's circular." They become critical of what they read, begin to question the author, and know that miscues aren't really mistakes but are evidence of their knowledge. In this way, exchanges between the teacher and the reader become more genuine.

As a result of our discussions, we become more comfortable with our responses as well. We ask questions to stimulate the conversation about selected miscues. None of the questions are meant to be used formulaically, and it is important to avoid the risk of turning sessions into a series of steps that become a set of boring procedures. Some questions are more useful than others, depending on the teacher's knowledge and experience and the age and confidence of the reader. And the more we engage in these conversations, the more sophisticated we become—both readers and teachers. Practice helps teachers become experts, and every new RMA session provides opportunities for more learning. As readers and teachers become comfortable and spontaneous with RMA, they rely less on the guiding RMA questions and more on their own expertise. Examples of questions often heard during RMA include:

- Why do you think you made that miscue?

- What do you think that (word, phrase, sentence, idea) means?

- What clues in the story/article allowed you to make this miscue?

- How does your miscue change the sentence/story/idea?

- Does that miscue affect your understanding of what you're reading?

- Did the miscue make the story/sentence/idea better?

- Why did you decide to keep going here? Did you have other options?

- Listen, and let's see if we hear the same thing again. (When the teacher and reader disagree about what they hear.)

- What have you learned about how you read and about yourself as a reader?

If students do not understand the questions, teachers rephrase them. Whenever possible, the focus of the discussion is on the positive nature of high-quality miscues and engages the reader in thinking about alternative strategies with low-quality miscues, always with the focus on making sense.

Here is an excerpt to show an interaction based on one selected miscue. Erica, a fifth grader, was considered a struggling reader according to teachers and test scores. She was a member of Gopa Goswami's fifth grade class, and Gopa and Erica worked together over a two year period. Erica listens to her miscue in our second RMA session.

0610 $^{66.}$ The wife

0611 stayed home to keep house and to look

0613 after their child.

Erica reads: *The wife stayed home to keep house and to look after their children, k-, kid, children.*

She makes three attempts to self-correct unsuccessfully, not producing the expected response. Her final reading is syntactically and semantically acceptable, with a partial meaning change from singular to plural. Code: **YYP**.

Gopa:	What did you do here?
Erica:	I read *children* and *kid*.
Gopa:	Do they fit the meaning of the story?
Erica:	No, because they only had one.
Gopa:	Does *kid* fit?
Erica:	No, because that's with a *k*.
Gopa:	What about the meaning?
Erica:	The meaning… it sounded good, but the picture and the story only had one little girl.

Gopa: Can the kid be a little girl?

Erica: Yeah.

Gopa: Why do you think you left it with *children* instead of *kid*?

Erica: Because it does start with *k*. *Children* sounded good… it couldn't be children, I said to myself, but I just kept reading.

Gopa: Do you know what you say for only one?

Erica: Kid…. Child? (with questioning intonation).

Gopa: Could that be child?

Erica: Yeah…. Cause *kid* didn't go with that story but *child* would.

Keep in mind that the major purpose of RMA sessions is to have genuine conversations with the reader—conversations that recognize, support, and build upon the reader's meaning-making strategies. Each time a miscue is examined, the reader is encouraged to explore *what happened*. Always keep the reader's comments in mind and follow her/his lead.

Preparing for Follow-Up Sessions

When the RMA session has ended, the teacher plans carefully for each of the subsequent sessions. The reader reads the new text aloud for RMI analysis and gives a retelling. The teacher then selects a new set of miscues for discussion. The RMI and RMA sessions continue in this cyclical manner. If the RMI and RMA sessions need to be conducted in the same day, it is helpful to have a break between them.

There is no prescription that dictates the number of RMA sessions that are needed. The number of sessions one might conduct depends on several factors: for one-on-one or small group mentoring, about six sessions over a two-month period are the minimum. When RMA is used in classroom settings, the overall concepts of thinking, talking, and revaluing about reading are revisited regularly whenever learners engage in literacy experiences (Y. Goodman, 2003; Y. Goodman & W. Goodman, 2011).

For one-on-one mentoring, the teacher uses RMI to analyze the reading and selects miscues for the subsequent session. Transcriptions or notes from previous sessions provide foundation for future planning. Keeping highlights of readers' responses throughout RMA provides information about the ways readers are shifting beliefs about reading and about themselves as readers. This evidence highlights the revaluing that results in ever-growing self-confidence. Such sessions work well with literacy volunteers or in English as a Second Language programs.

In subsequent sessions, students are encouraged to bring their own reading materials, which are photocopied for marking purposes, unless the teacher has a preplanned set of familiar materials with typescripts ready for markings. If there are interesting miscues left from previous discussions, subsequent RMA sessions can include those miscues, and the reading of a new selection may be postponed. Taking into consideration the intensity of the RMA session, students' responses, and their ages, proficiencies, and confidence, teachers rephrase or ask new questions. Students are also encouraged to formulate their own questions and wonder about ways to think about their reading.

Part III
Students Working Together:
Organizing Alternative RMA Sessions

RMA is flexible and adaptable. We have used RMA for reading instruction with a wide range of learners. We teach RMA for undergraduate and graduate students working toward specialties in reading and for those who will be teaching reading to students in elementary and secondary schools. RMA is used successfully with adults working on their high school GEDs, in adult literacy programs, and with second language learners. Readers become especially enthusiastic when they discover that the major purpose of reading is for them to make sense and that they already use many productive reading strategies.

Gina, a 41-year-old adult diagnosed as a dyslexic throughout her schooling, considered herself a nonreader. She worked with Ann Alexander (Marek) (1996) in a number of tutoring sessions. This first excerpt is from their second RMA session, and the next is from a session two months later. Gina believed strongly that a reader was obliged to read what was in the written text. By comparing early and later RMA sessions, we see Gina's shift from believing in the primacy of the text over her own meaning making to believing she has the right to interpret texts as she reads. In the first excerpt, she read the following sentence substituting *transport* for *transportation*.

Despite the fact that air travel remains,

transport
by far, our safest form of transportation,

we asked, "Is it safe to fly?"

This high-quality miscue results in a syntactically and semantically acceptable sentence with no meaning change. Code: **YYN**.

Ann: Does your miscue produce a semantically acceptable sentence?

Gina: I would have said it right if I'd looked at it hard enough.

Here is an excerpt from Gina during an RMA session a few months later:

All I have to do is $\overset{to}{\underset{\wedge}{}}$ sit here.

Gina: (after listening to her taping, she reads aloud and responds) *All I have to do is sit here.* Yes, I would say *to sit here.*

Ann: Do you need to correct it?

Gina: No.

Ann: Why do you think you are making these miscues? Why do you say *housekeeping* instead of *keeping house,* leave out *so,* insert *to*?

Gina: Really, what I am doing is taking this story into my hands a bit. Whether a schoolteacher would correct it or not I don't know.

Classroom teachers use RMA as a tool for organizing guided reading lessons and involving small groups of students working collaboratively in exploring their own reading processes. When Alan Flurkey taught primary grades, he would walk around the room when students were engaged in silent reading (Y. Goodman, 1996, p. 608). He would stop at children's desks and ask them to keep reading but to read aloud so he could hear them and talk with them about how they read. One day, he stopped at Maureen's desk. She read:

$\overset{\text{(c)}}{}$ As he turned the corner he $\overset{was}{\underline{saw}}$ the lion.

Maureen: *As he turned the corner he was … As he turned the corner he saw the lion.*

Alan's notes show that Maureen made an apparent prediction, stopped, regressed to the beginning of the sentence, and then read the sentence as expected. Alan waited until she came to the end of the page and revisited what he saw and heard.

Alan: I noticed that near the top of the page you stopped, backed up, and then continued to read. I'm wondering what you were thinking about.

Maureen: You mean up here?

Alan: Yes.

Maureen: Well, when I got to the middle of the sentence, it didn't make sense so I just started over.

Alan: What didn't make sense?

Maureen: Well I thought it was going to say, like, "he was scared … was scared of what was there…"

Alan: So then what did you do?

Maureen: It didn't say that, so I just started over.

Alan summarized for Maureen that she was using predicting, confirming, and self-correcting strategies; that she was clearly aware of how and when she was using these strategies; and that she was able to discuss her reading with him with confidence. Teachers engage in such over-the-shoulder miscues as part of their reading instruction supporting readers in many settings in the classroom (Davenport & Lauritzen, 2002). In the preceding sections, we describe RMA with one student, while in the next section, we suggest RMA for alternate venues.

Collaborative RMA

Collaborative Retrospective Miscue Analysis (CRMA) is a variation of RMA that works well with small groups of students, fifth grade through high school age (Costello, 1996; Moore & Gilles, 2008). The teacher organizes sessions for four to five students to work together two to three times a week for about 30 minutes and discuss the reading miscues of one of their group. One reader agrees to be recorded reading aloud. Later, the other members mark miscues, listen to the reader's retelling, and discuss the reader's miscues using RMA procedures and questions.

Once the student volunteer's reading and retelling have been recorded, the CRMA session can begin. Procedures and questions similar to the ones suggested for one-on-one RMA are often printed for the students to follow. One participant or the teacher starts a second recorder while the group listens to the original reading on the first recorder, following along with the original text or a typescript. The second recorder provides evidence of the discussion to verify disagreements that arise. The typescript may or may not have miscues marked, depending upon the teacher's purposes.

When the miscues are already marked by the teacher, especially early in the use of CRMA, it can facilitate discussion. However, as readers become more experienced, they learn a lot as they discuss their miscue markings together. While listening to the first recording, as many times as necessary, readers mark miscues on their own typescripts that they then discuss with their peers. It is useful to have a heterogeneous group of students working together so readers of all proficiencies appreciate that all readers make miscues, use strategies similar to their own, and are capable of talking about reading and literacy processes.

Students working together highlight the powerful social nature of learning. In CRMA, the teacher works collaboratively with the students during the beginning sessions and demonstrates the possible directions CRMA sessions can take (Costello, 1996). Eventually, the students run the CRMA sessions themselves, with the teacher present for a short time acting as a consultant. Some teachers attend the end of the session or plan a regular conference with the students to monitor what they are gaining from the experience and to help deepen their notions about reading. Teachers sit in on CRMA sessions to assure that the experience continues to be positive and dynamic. Literacy volunteers working with adults find that such grouping also works well with adult learners.

Whole Class RMA in Middle and High Schools

Some English or language arts teachers hold CRMA-like sessions with a whole class as part of a theme study on the nature of reading and writing and the role of literacy practices in their lives. They involve students in researching their literacy practices by doing "literacy digs" of their backpacks (an anthropological-type "excavation" of all the kinds of written language in one's possession) or making lists of all the literacy that they notice for a specific period of time to discover where and how literacy practices take place in their homes or communities (D. Goodman, 1999; Y. Goodman, 2003; Taylor, 1993). They explore how signs are used to control marketing and urban planning in their communities. The teacher engages them in explorations of nonsense poems like *Jabberwocky* by Lewis Carroll (Caroll & Tenniel, 1999, pp. 10-12) or passages with embedded miscues like *The Boat in the Basement* by Kenneth Goodman (1996, p. 38) to talk about the reading process. Students compare such readings with how they think they read familiar and interesting material. In some classes, students explore miscues in their reading of headlines or signs in the environment.

Students then participate in a miscue analysis on one of their peers' reading. The teacher asks a student volunteer to read aloud as the other students record the reading and mark miscues. They learn how to <u>mark miscues</u> and <u>to analyze</u> <u>them using the miscue analysis</u> questions (see pp. 21-24). For class purposes, one reading may be sufficient, but some teachers involve many students in such oral readings so that they eventually become comfortable reading for their peers.

As students develop greater understanding of miscues, teachers involve them in considering how different types of miscues are helpful as they read. Teachers may focus class attention on particular kinds of miscues, i.e., omissions that result in semantically and syntactically acceptable sentences, or proper name substitutions. And they begin to discuss reading strategies such as rereading or reading ahead, considering when such strategies are useful or not. In this way, the RMA session becomes a reading strategy (Y. Goodman et al., 1996) or mini lesson (Atwell, 2002).

RMA with Young Children

Beginning readers are developing knowledge and building concepts about reading from their earliest encounter with printed texts (D. Goodman, Flurkey, & Y. Goodman, 2007). Since young children are very capable of talking and thinking about reading and the reading process, we recommend discussions about reading during over-the-shoulder conversations or during instructional periods such as guided reading.

Wendy Goodman provides an example from her first grade (Y. Goodman & W. Goodman, 2011). The children in this heterogeneous guided reading group are reading *Ask Mr. Bear* by Marjorie Flack (1958). They each have a copy of the book in front of them and, although encouraged to read silently, they tend to read aloud, sometimes simultaneously. In the following example, the children are reading page 3 of the story and come to the following sentence:

I can give you a nice fresh egg for your mother's birthday.

The children read: I can give you a nice … (they pause) … Wendy asks them to place a finger on *that word* [fresh] and keep reading. The kids do so and continue: "I can give you a nice egg for your mother's birthday." Wendy says, "Do you need that word there?" and most of the group says "no."

Shawn: But it's there. We need to read it.

Wendy: What kind of an egg could it be?

Emma: Free.

Fatima: Fresh?

Claudia: Fresh?

Kids: Oh, yeah … fresh egg.

Wendy: Does that make sense?

The children review the experience, agree that *fresh egg* makes sense in the sentence, and quickly continue reading. Wendy uses similar discussions during her guided reading, taking into consideration the children's miscues and the strategies they use in their responses to the text. Their discussion also covers the content, the characters, and the illustrations, always focusing on making sense.

Teachers involved with RMA are well aware of the negative attitudes that some of their students have about themselves as readers. As we've said, it is not uncommon to hear readers declare that they are poor readers. When discussing their perceptions of their own reading, or when asked during an RMA session why they made a particular miscue, they say "Oh, I messed up," "I wasn't paying attention," "I always leave out words," "I was reading too fast," "I don't know all the words," "I should have looked up the words in the dictionary," " I put in different words," "I didn't stop at the 'stop sign'," or "I read too slow," These readers often say they hate reading and avoid it as much as they can.

Research on RMA makes it clear that readers are eager to explore why they make miscues and use that evidence to revalue themselves as readers as they become consciously aware that the behaviors they thought were *their problems* involve reading strategies that all readers engage in. As a result, they develop self-confidence and reach out to participate in the "literacy club" (Smith, 1988) to which their parents, friends, and teachers already belong. It is to this end that we encourage the use of RMA.

Not all readers immediately become avid readers as a result of the RMA experiences, but all readers revalue themselves and develop greater confidence as literate members of society. They still may not like reading, but they are more willing to use reading to solve the problems they have, to make their lives and their work in a literate society richer and easier. As a result, they read more and continue to develop their reading abilities. There is nothing more important to continuous growth as a reader than to read widely in diverse and interesting materials, including all the emerging digital media.

Teachers also continue their professional development as a result of engaging in RMA and expand on their understandings as they continue to read what other professionals working with RMA and miscue analysis are thinking and doing. We encourage you to look through the references that follow, and visit the Essential RMA website, www.retrospectivemiscue.com. As these resources stimulate your interest in RMA, please let us know how you use these ideas and what questions and concerns you have, and share your progress and adaptations with us.

Yetta M. Goodman, **ygoodman@u.arizona.edu**
Prisca Martens, **pmartens@towson.edu**
Alan D. Flurkey, **alan.d.flurkey@hofstra.edu**
www.retrospectivemiscue.com

Appendix A:
Burke Reading Interview (BRI)

Name _____ Age _____ Date _____ Sex _____

Occupation _____ Education Level ____ Interview Setting _____

1. When you're reading and you come to something you don't know, what do you do?

    Do you ever do anything else?

2. Who is a good reader that you know?

3. What makes _____ a good reader?

4. Do you think _____ ever comes to something they don't know?

5. "Yes" When _____ does come to something she/he doesn't know, what do you think he/she does?

    "No" Suppose _____ comes to something she/he doesn't know. What would she/he do?

6. How would you help someone having difficulty reading?

7. What would a/your teacher do to help that person?

8. How did you learn to read?

9. What would you like to do better as a reader?

    Do you think you are a good reader? Why?

For readers who live in bilingual or multilingual communities or households, it is important to gather information about their reading in their various languages. Ask readers: "Do you ever see or read any materials in languages other than English?" Probe to remind the readers that they might read newspapers and signs in the environment or on food packages, as well as letters or text messages from relatives or businesses in other countries, etc.

Goodman, Y., Watson, D., & Burke, C. (2005). *Reading miscue inventory: From evaluation to instruction* (pp. 273-274). New York: Richard C. Owen.

Appendix B:
Burke Interview Modified for Older Readers (BIMOR)

Name _____ Age _____ Date _____ Sex _____

Occupation _____ Education Level ____ Interview Setting _____

1. When you're reading and you come to something you don't know, what do you do?

   Do you ever do anything else?

2. Who is a good reader that you know?

3. What makes _____ a good reader?

4. Do you think _____ ever comes to something that gives him/her trouble when he/she is reading?

5. When _____ does come to something that gives him/her trouble, what do you think he/she does about it

6. How would you help someone having difficulty reading?

7. What would a teacher do to help that person?

8. How did you learn to read?

9. Is there anything you would like to change about your reading?

10. Describe yourself as a reader: What kind of reader are you?

11. What do you read routinely, like every day or every week?

12. What do you like most of all to read?

13. Can you remember any special book or the most memorable thing you have ever read?

14. What is the most difficult thing you have to read?

For readers who live in bilingual or multilingual communities or households, it is important to gather information about their reading in their various languages. Ask readers: "Do you ever see or read any materials in languages other than English?" Probe to remind the readers that they might read newspapers and signs in the environment or on food packages, as well as letters or text messages from relatives or businesses in other countries, etc.

Goodman, Y., Watson, D., & Burke, C. (2005). *Reading miscue inventory: From evaluation to instruction* (pp. 273-274). New York: Richard C. Owen.

Appendix C:
Entrevista Burke
(Burke Reading Interview in Spanish)

Nombre _____ Edad _____ Fecha _____ Sexo _____

Oficio _____ Nivel Educativo _____ Interview Setting _____

Marco de la Entrevista Interview Setting _____

1. Cuando usted está leyendo y encuentra algo que no sabe ¿qué hace?

2. ¿Alguna vez a hecho algo más?

3. ¿Quién es un buen lector que usted conoce?

4. ¿Qué hace a _____ un buen lector?

5. ¿Usted cree que alguna vez _____ encontró algo que no sabe?

6. Si es "sí," cuando _____ encuentra algo que no sabe, ¿Qué cree que hace?

7. Si es "no," supongamos que _____ encuentra algo que no sabe, ¿Qué cree que haría?

8. Si usted supiera de alguien que está teniendo problemas para leer, ¿Cómo ayudaría a esa persona?

9. ¿Qué debería hacer el maestro para ayudar le a esa persona?

10. ¿Cómo aprendió a leer?

11. ¿Qué le gustaría mejorar como lector?

12. ¿Cree que es un buen lector? ¿Por qué si o por qué no?

Translated from: Goodman, Y., Watson, D., & Burke, C. (2005). *Reading miscue inventory: From evaluation to instruction* (pp. 273-274). New York: Richard C. Owen. Translators Consuelo B. Carrillo and Richard Ruiz

Appendix D:
Selecting texts for RMI and RMA

by Alan D. Flurkey and Debra Goodman

Finding and selecting appropriate materials for personal and instructional reading for RMI and RMA purposes takes a great deal of knowledge about the readers and the uses for the material. The selection of reading materials for the purposes of evaluation and instruction should be central in discussions about RMI and RMA. Teachers and students should be consciously aware of this important aspect of reading. It is useful to hold discussions in teacher education programs, among all the teachers involved and the students throughout the grades, about the importance of thoughtful selection of reading material that is of interest to and serves the needs of readers.

In relation to selecting materials, we use concepts of accessibility as well as focusing on natural, predictable, familiar, and complex language. These terms need to be considered based on knowing as much as possible about the reader and how these concepts relate to readers' background knowledge, experiences, interests and capabilities.

Choice

Avid readers spend time selecting materials that are right for their purposes. They know which bookstores that have selections they like. They frequent libraries and other places where books and magazines are plentiful. The books and magazines that avid readers would purchase for themselves should be offered to all students as well. Classroom, school and community libraries should be rich with a range of print and digital materials.

Visiting reading recovery sites in New Zealand, Yetta was part of a textbook selection experience that involved classroom teachers. The teachers were sitting at a large table piled with recently published books. Teachers working collaboratively based on the age of their students or the content/subject matter areas they taught read and selected books for their classroom and school libraries. As they read, they began to categorize the features of the books they thought would be best for their students. These criteria became the rubrics used to establish a sense of readability for the books. They developed their own labels to represent the difficulty of the books. Later in their classrooms, some teachers worked in a similar vein with their students and even developed their own labels. In this way, the students were better able to understand the teachers' categories and the issues surrounding what makes reading material hard or easy.

Some classroom libraries had books organized on shelves labeled *Easy to Read*, *Just Right*, and *A Challenge but Worth It*. Being involved in such an experience lead students to understand why libraries have categories for book selection and how different categorical systems have been organized over the years. Librarians are invited to discuss these issues with students.

Readability formulas have been developed by individual scholars and publishing companies over the years to support teachers and parents in selecting material for students. In order to be computerized, such formulas have included simplistic information such as the number of words and sentences, the ratio of hard words to easy words, the number of syllables in words, etc. These formulas provide some information but do not focus on the two aspects of book selection that are most important to learners: how the material relates to what the individual reader is interested in and how the material relates to the knowledge and capability of the reader to allow connections between the reader's background and the content of the material.

Material to Answer Questions Raised by the Student and/or by Assignments

When we first started working with teachers, we provided lists of children's books that related to students' interests. We stopped doing that when we discovered that there were so many such lists available on the Internet. For example, when one student or a group of students want to know about basketball, we can use the Internet to find basketball reading lists or children's literature on friendship.

Developmental Interest

Based on teachers' and students' intuition and experience it is possible to determine if the story or content is likely to appeal to readers. Texts are selected that focus on topics or characters of interest to the students and appropriate for the age group. A picture book with humor or irony may be a good selection for older students who need an "easier" text. Many picture books, especially in the content areas, have sophisticated information about science, history, and other subject matter that older students find useful. A younger child who is reading at a more "advanced" level still needs a topic or plot appropriate for his/her age group. Adolescents don't tend to enjoy stories as much if they are about older adults.

Predictability:

Texts that contain natural story language, that have inviting illustrations, and that are interesting and meaningful for the reader tend to be more predictable and accessible. Keep in mind the things in each of the following areas that make texts more for predictable for the reader:

- Language

- Experience/conceptual background

- Interest

- Meaningfulness for the reader

- Illustration, diagrams, photos, etc.

Personal Preference:

Interview students or students can interview each other to discover how they respond to the following aspects of the texts for selection:

- Genre

- Topic

- Style

- Media (is reading on a tablet, laptop or phone preferred over paper books or magazines?)

Texts That Typically Work Well:

- Picture books

- Complete short stories

- Informative articles on relevant topics

- Folk tales with several concrete events

- Plays that might lend themselves to collaborative RMA

Texts That Don't Typically Work Well for Miscue Analysis (especially for the initial sessions):

- Book chapters. A chapter excepted from a book is usually not suitable, especially when it occurs later in a book. Book chapters generally don't "stand alone" because there are often too many characters who may have been introduced in earlier chapters, or events that are mentioned and not explained that are relevant to the meaning. All things considered, whole, stand-alone texts work best.

- Texts that rhyme

- Abridged texts

- Unfamiliar topics

- Texts only about adult characters used with young children

- Controlled vocabulary texts ("artificial" texts written solely for instructional purposes)

Supports and Challenges:

- Readers may find reading uninteresting and less engaging if the text does not offer any sort of challenge to them. When selecting a text, the idea is to strike a balance between the aspects of texts that "support" meaning construction and those that "challenge" a reader just enough to push a reader slightly beyond the comfort level (Clay, 1972; Y. Goodman, 1982; Mooney, 2004).

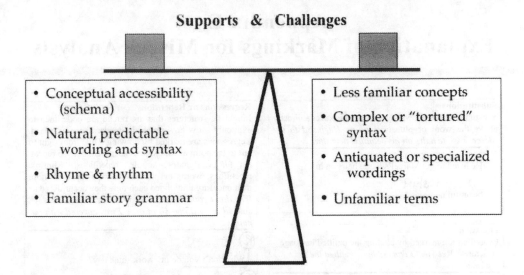

It is useful to involve the readers in discussions about selecting books related to the above categories and to expand on the categories. This provides teachers with greater insight into the selection process

Appendix E:
Explanation of Markings for Miscue Analysis

Substitutions
Substitutions are shown by writing the miscue directly above the word or phrase. Read as *He hated to get Marcel's white hairs on his beautiful new shirt.*

He hated to get Marcel's white hairs on his

shirt

beautiful new suit.

Omission
Omissions are marked by circling the omitted language structures. Read as *"I can do that," replied the husband.*

"I can do (all) that," replied the husband.

Insertions
Insertions are shown by marking a proofreader's caret at the point of insertion and writing the inserted word or phrase where it occurs in the text. Read as *"Now I've got some more work to do," said the man.*

some
"Now I've got more work to do," said the man.
∧

Regressing and Abandoning a Correct Form
Abandonments are marked by drawing a line from right to left at the point at which the reader went back to repeat but abandoned the expected text. An (AC) is used to indicate this type of regression. In this example, the reader first reads *head against the wall*, then rejects this possibility and produces the more sensible *hand against the wall*. Read as *"How many times did I hit my head against the wall—hand against the wall?" she asked.*

(AC) hand
"How many times did I hit my head against the

wall?" she asked.

Regressions or Repetitions
Linguistic structures that are reread are underlined to explicitly show how much the reader chose to reread. Regressions are marked by drawing a line from right to left to the point at which the reader went back to repeat. An (R) designates simple repetitions. Multiple repetitions, words or phrases that are repeated more than once, are underlined each time they occur. Read as *Why don't you—Why don't you do my work some day?* and *All at—All at—All at once I was covered with red paint.*

(R)
Why don't you do my work some day?

(R)
All at once I was covered with red paint.

Regressing and Correcting the Miscue (self-corrections)
Self-corrections are marked by drawing a line from right to left to the point at which the reader went back to repeat in order to correct the miscue. A (c) indicates a correction.

The markings in this example show that the reader substitutes *flash* for the words *few minutes*. She then regresses and corrects the miscue: *I'll light a fire in the fireplace and the porridge will be ready in a flash—a few minutes.*

I'll light a fire in the fireplace and the porridge will

(c) flash
be ready in a few minutes.

Substitutions Often Called Reversals
An editor's transposition symbol shows which words have been reversed. Read as *I sat down looking at Andrew.* and *Something was wrong with Papa.*

I sat looking down at Andrew.

Was something wrong with Papa?

Regressing and Unsuccessfully Attempting to Correct

Unsuccessful attempts to correct are marked by drawing a line from right to left to the point at which the reader began to repeat in an attempt to correct. A (UC) is used to designate this type of regression.

In this example, the reader says *river washed* twice and this is marked as (UC), an unsuccessful attempt at correction. Read as *And this he did with such might that soon the river washed—river washed over its banks,...*

And this he did with such might that soon the

(UC) washed

river rushed over its banks,...

Nonword Substitutions

A dollar sign ($) indicates that a reader has produced a miscue that is not recognizable as a word in the reader's language. Retain as much of the original spelling of the text word as possible. Read as *Judy shrickled and jumped up in her chair.*

$shrickled

Judy shrieked and jumped up in her chair.

Partial Miscues

Partial miscues are marked by putting a dash after a partial word when a reader attempts but does not produce a complete word. Intonation is used to determine partial miscues.

Often readers start to say a word and self-correct or attempt a correction before a word is completed. Here, the reader predicts *ability*. He only starts the word and immediately self-corrects to *able*. Partial attempts that are corrected are marked on the typescript with a dash following the partial, but are not transferred to the coding sheet.

There is nothing greater than man and the work

abi-

he is best able to do.

Repeated Miscues

Repeated miscues are marked with an (RM) to indicate the same miscue for the same text item.

come   come   (RM)

Off came our boots. Off came our socks.

Intonation Shift

An accent mark indicates intonation shifts within a word. Intonation shifts are marked only if there is a change in meaning or grammatical structure of the original text.

He will récord her voice.

We want the próject to succeed.

Pauses

A $\mathcal{P}$ marks noticeable pauses in reading. It is useful to mark the length of unusually long pauses.

$\mathcal{P}$ 23 sec.

"What do you do all day while I am away cutting

wood?"

Dialect and Other Language Variations

Miscues that involve a sound, vocabulary item, or grammatical variation that is perceived as a dialect difference between the author and reader are marked with a (d). Read as *I switched off the headlights of the car... and ...just about everybody like babies.*

headlights (d)

I switched off the headlamps of the car...

like   (d)

...just about everybody likes babies.

Appendix F:
Examples of Oral Asides, Subvocalizing, Perusal of Illustrations, and Finger Pointing

Oral asides from Ian's reading of *The Sweetest Fig* (Van Allsburg, 1993)

0609 set the figs down and took her by the arm. [23.] When she *Then*	22. _____
0610 reminded him about the pills, he said, "I'm sorry, only *. He*	
0611 for paying customers," and shoved her out the door. 23. _____	

"*Which is pretty bad.*"

2002   he was. [52.] As he slept, the dentist saw himself
2003   steering his speedboat, flying his aeroplane,
2004   and living in luxury on the Riviera. [53.] Night *river*
2005   after night it was the same.

"*And aeroplane is spelled like aeroplane, so don't miscue me on that.*"

Subvocalizations during Daniel's reading of *Winnie the Witch* (Thomas & Paul, 2007)

13:43

1301b   28. Winnie came hurrying outside,

hur-ρ
c-
hurry— ← *sounds out under breath — uses "word attack skills."*

14:15

1501   29. This time, Winnie was furious.   29. _____

$furous
furi-
fur- }
ρ16

→ *Note prediction and correction*
← *Note graphophonic strengths*

whispered   *voiced aloud*
5. "(I can't s-) It's hard. I'll skip it."
4. fúrous
3. "I can't say that word." ρ16s → *laughs to self and whispers to self*
2. fyŏor-ĭ-
1. fyŏor

1502   30. She picked up her magic wand,

16:28

1901   35. Wilbur climbed to the top of the tallest tree to hide.   35. _____

c clim-

→ *whispers to self during pause, presumably to attempt to use graphophonic cues*

1902   36. He looked ridiculous and he knew it.   36. _____

ρ16s

15:09

ρ5s.

1701   (...ABRACADABRA!) 31. Wilbur had a red head,   30. _____

→ ρ5 "I can't say that..." ρ5x "...really can't..."

18:15

2102   44. She waved her magic wand and

*That's..weird words"
(no significant pause here)*

2103   (ABRACADABRA!) 45. Wilbur was a   44. _____

Oral asides and perusals of illustrations during Daniel's reading of *The Sweetest Fig* (Van Allsburg, 1993). Teacher notes below were compiled after the reading.

Sent #	Sentence	page pause duration (sec)	Comments before the reading begins on this page:
4	Except on Bastille Day, the poor animal was not even allowed to bark.	11.4	Daniel begins to read to himself. When he starts to turn the page, I redirect him, saying, "Pardon? Could you go back—and I didn't hear this one—Could you go back and reread this one 'cause you started reading to yourself."
24	That evening, Bibot took his little dog to the park.	16.3	Daniel takes a long look at page 6 illustration.
37	The dentist turned and ran into an alley.	34.7	Daniel (aside) looking at page 11: "Is that enough for you? Now looking at page 13, turning pages back and forth: "I didn't see him get his dog. Where'd he get his dog? 'Cause in the picture (11), he's not there with the dog." (Turns to page 13) "And now look, he's with the dog." Alan: "Huh...huh! Interesting. Yeah, I never noticed that."
38	"Sacré bleu," he thought.	5.22	Daniel: "I don't know what that word is. It's French."
41	In his dream, he'd stood in front of that very café, dressed in his underwear.	6.3	Daniel: "So she *did* te- say the truth."
49	Over the next few weeks, as reconstruction of the Eiffel Tower began, the dentist read dozens of books of hypnotism.	23.8	Daniel: "What time do I have to go?" Alan: "Um, probably in about 10 more minutes. We're almost done with the story."

62	As the dentist reached into his cupboard to take out some cheese, he heard the crash of breaking china.	46.9	Daniel momentarily stops reading to comment on the story.
			Daniel: "He's (Marcel) gonna take it, and then he's (Bibot) gonna fly with him (Marcel)."
			Alan: "What?"
			Daniel: "The dog's gonna take it (the fig) and then he'll (Bibot) go with him. So he's (the dog) smart. He said, "Now—" He doesn't want him to go with him, so he's gonna eat it. Then he'll go with him."
			Alan: "Is that your prediction? Okay. How's that—How's the dog gonna go with him if he eats it? What's…"
			Daniel: "If he eats it, then if *he* dreams and the dentist dreams, then probably he'll—dog will have the same dream as him and then he'll go with him."
			Alan: "Wait and see."

Appendix G1:
RMA Session Organizer

Reader_____

Date_____

Text_____

Miscue Number	Tape Recorder Counter Number	Line Number	Miscue	+/-
____	____	____	_____	
____	____	____	_____	
____	____	____	_____	
____	____	____	_____	
____	____	____	_____	
____	____	____	_____	
____	____	____	_____	
____	____	____	_____	

Notes:

Goodman, Y., & Marek, A. (1996). *Retrospective miscue analysis: Revaluing readers and reading* (p. 211). Katonah, NY: Richard C. Owen.

Appendix G2:
Session Organizer for Daniel's RMA

Reader_____ **Daniel**

Date_____ December 18, 2008

Text_____ *Winnie the Witch*

Miscue Number	Tape-Recorder Counter Number	Line Number	Miscue	+/-
1	12:23	1006	He was ^a bright green.	*insertion*
2	12:23	1102	Winnie ^can could see him.	*substitution*
3	12:40	1104	Winnie ^can could see him.	*substitution*
4	11:40	0503	She could see his eyes⟨on⟩anyway.	*prediction / correction*
5	11:00	0604	So⟨the⟩she sat on him.	p/c
6	18:15	2103	(ABRACADABRA)	*How did you deal with this*
7	18:15	2104	…was a black cat once⟨ag-⟩more.	p/c
8	18:15	2105	He ^can come came down from the tree purring.	*subst.*
9	09:20	0105	The ⟨uc⟩ carpets were black.	*Repeated miscue*
10	11:13	0701	When Wilbur sat on the carpet with his eyes open, Winnie…	*ER*

produces the expected response of "carpet" the 3rd time it appears

References

Atwell, N. (2002). *Lessons that change writers.* Portsmouth, NH: Firsthand.

Brown, J., Goodman, K., & Marek, A. (1996). *Studies in miscue analysis: An annotated bibliography.* Newark, DE: International Reading Association.

Carroll, L., & Tenniel, J. (1999). *Through the looking-glass and what Alice found there.* Mineola, NY: Dover Publications.

Clay, M. (1972). *The early detection of reading difficulties.* London: Heinemann Educational Books.

Costello, S. (1996). A teacher/researcher uses RMA. In Y. Goodman & A. Marek (Eds.), *Retrospective Miscue Analysis: Revaluing readers and reading* (pp. 165-175). Katonah, NY: Richard C. Owen Publishers, Inc.

Davenport, M. R., & Lauritzen, C. (2002). Inviting reflection on reading through over the shoulder miscue analysis. *Language Arts, 80*(2), 109–118.

Duckett, P. (2007). *Cleaning grandma's attic: Reading strategies.* Paper presented at National Council of Teachers of English Annual Convention, New York, NY.

Flack, M. (1958). *Ask Mr. Bear.* New York, NY: Macmillan.

Flurkey, A. (1996). Revaluing and revelations. In Y. Goodman & A. Marek (Eds.), *Retrospective miscue analysis: Revaluing readers and reading.* (pp. 107-118). Katonah, NY: Richard C. Owen Publishers, Inc.

Goodman, D. (1999). *The reading detective club.* Portsmouth, NH: Heinemann.

Goodman, D., Flurkey, A., & Goodman, Y. (2007). Effective young beginning readers. In Y. Goodman & P. Martens (Eds.), *Critical issues in early literacy: Research and pedagogy* (pp. 3–16). Abingdon, England: Routledge.

Goodman, K. (1973). Miscues: Windows on the reading process. In K. Goodman (Ed.), *Miscue Analysis: Applications to reading instruction* (3-14). Urbana, IL: Eric Clearing House on Reading and Communication Skills. Also in A. Flurkey & J. Xu (Eds.), *On the revolution of reading: The selected writings of Kenneth S. Goodman* (pp. 107-116). Portsmouth, NH: Heinemann.

Goodman, K. (1996). *On reading*. Portsmouth, NH: Heinemann.

Goodman, K. (2003/2014). Revaluing readers and reading. In A. Flurkey & J. Xu (Eds.), *On the revolution of reading: The selected writings of Kenneth S. Goodman* (pp. 421-429). Also in K. Goodman, & Y. Goodman (Eds). *Making sense of learners making sense of written language: The selected works of Kenneth S. Goodman and Yetta M. Goodman* (pp. 189-196). New York, NY: Routledge.

Goodman, K., & Goodman, Y. (2011/2014). Learning to read: A comprehensive model. In R. Meyer & K. Whitmore (Eds.), *Reclaiming reading: Teachers, students and researchers regaining spaces for thinking and action* (pp. 19–41). New York: Taylor & Francis. *Also* in Goodman, K., & Goodman, Y. (Eds.), *Making sense of learners making sense of written language: The selected works of Kenneth S. Goodman and Yetta M. Goodman* (pp. 56–74). New York, NY: Routledge.

Goodman, K., & Goodman, Y. (2014). *Making sense of learners making sense of written language: The selected works of Kenneth S. Goodman and Yetta M. Goodman*. New York, NY: Routledge.

Goodman, Y. (1982). Retellings of literature and the comprehension process. *Theory into Practice, 21*(4), 300–307.

Goodman, Y. (1996). Revaluing readers while readers revalue themselves: Retrospective miscue analysis. *Reading Teacher, 49*(8), 600–609.

Goodman, Y. (2003). *Valuing language study: Inquiry into language for elementary and middle schools*. Urbana, IL: National Council of Teachers of English.

Goodman, Y., & Goodman, W. (2011/2014). Eager young readers, a well constructed text and an insightful teacher. *NERA Journal, 46*(2) 9–16. Also in K. Goodman, & Y. Goodman. (Eds.), *Making sense of learners making sense of written language: The selected works of Kenneth S. Goodman and Yetta M. Goodman* (pp. 222–234). New York, NY: Routledge.

Goodman, Y., & Marek, A. (1996). *Retrospective miscue analysis: Revaluing readers and reading*. Katonah, NY: Richard C. Owen Publishers, Inc.

Goodman, Y., Watson, D., & Burke, C. (1996). *Reading strategies: Focus on comprehension*. Katonah, NY: Richard C. Owen Publishers, Inc.

Goodman, Y., Watson, D., & Burke, C. (2005). *Reading miscue inventory: From Evaluation to Instruction*. Katonah, NY: Richard C. Owen Publishers, Inc.

Martens, P., Goodman, Y., & Flurkey, A. (1995). Miscue analysis for classroom teachers: Some history and some procedures. *Primary Voices, 4*(3), 2–9.

Meek, M. (1988). *How texts teach what readers learn*. Stroud, England: Thimble Press. Available in the US from Richard C. Owen Publishers, Inc.

Menosky, D. M. (1971). *A psycholinguistic analysis of oral reading miscues generated during the reading of varying portions of text by selected readers from grades two, four, six, and eight: A descriptive study* (Ph.D. dissertation). Retrieved from ERIC database. (ED067618)

Mooney, M. (2004). *A book is a present: Selecting text for intentional teaching*. Katonah, NY: Richard C. Owen Publishers, Inc.

Moore, R., & Gilles, C. (2008). *Reading conversations: Retrospective miscue analysis with struggling readers, grades 4–12*. Portsmouth, NH: Heinemann.

Nelson, R., Damico, J., & Smith, S. (2006). Applying eye movement miscue analysis to the reading patterns of children with language impairment. *Clinical Linguistics & Phonetics, 22*(4), 293–303.

Siegel, M. (1991). *Reading as signification*. London, England: Falmer Press.

Smith, F. (1988). *Joining the literacy club: Further essays into education*. Portsmouth, NH: Heinemann.

Smith, F. (1995). *Between hope and havoc: Essays into human learning and education* (pp. 1–13). Portsmouth, NH: Heinemann.

Taylor, D. (1993). *From the child's point of view*. Portsmouth, NH: Heinemann.

Thomas, V., & Paul, K. (2007). *Winnie the witch*. New York, NY: Harpercollins.

Van Allsburg, C. (1993). *The sweetest fig*. Boston, MA: Houghton-Mifflin.

Whitin, P. (1996). *Sketching stories, stretching minds: Responding visually to literature*. Portsmouth, NH: Heinemann.

Whitmore, K., Martens, P., Goodman, Y., & Owocki, G. (2005). Remembering critical lessons in early literacy research: A transactional perspective. *Language Arts, 82*(4), 296–307.

Index

About the Authors

Yetta M. Goodman, Regents Professor Emerita, University of Arizona, supports teachers as professional observers of learners (kidwatchers) and innovative curriculum developers in collaboration with their students. She publishes about miscue analysis and the constructivist nature of literacy learning and teaching and holds leadership positions in literacy organizations. Contact Yetta at ygoodman@u.arizona.edu.

Prisca Martens is a Professor in the Department of Elementary Education at Towson University, Towson, Maryland, where she teaches courses on reading/literacy and children's literature. Her research and publications are in the areas of early literacy, miscue analysis, retrospective miscue analysis, and children's literature. She can be reached at pmartens@towson.edu.

Alan D. Flurkey is Associate Professor of Literacy Studies in the School of Education at Hofstra University. He has taught elementary grades and special education classes and he has directed the Reading/Writing Learning Clinic. His research interests include RMA, eye-movement miscue analysis, studies of reading proficiency, and applications of corpus linguistics. Alan's email address is alan.d.flurkey@hofstra.edu.